30 RITUALS OF HIGHLY SUCCESSFUL PEOPLE

*THE FAST TRACK METHOD THAT
WILL HELP YOU SUCCEED IN LIFE*

KRISHNA MEDGE

First Edition: December, 2017

ISBN-13:

978-1981728824

ISBN-10:

1981728821

Printed In The United States of America

ACKNOWLEDGEMENT

To my family and friends, I am very glad for giving me your full support and guidance in other to make this project come through.

To my book editor: Katherine Thomas, Margaret Cobb, and Richard Smith. Thanks for taking time to lay this out and providing me the inspiration to do this. Thank you guys and i appreciate you more than you will ever know.

To my book designer: Rebecca, you brought my book to life and gave me a target to write to, and visual to start conversation and prime the promotion pump

To my proofreaders: Amy R. Alderson, Melinda S. Davidson and all others who took the time to help me find some needed corrections and error to my book. Thanks guys and i really appreciate your effort.

To you: who wish to better yourself by taking time to read this book; you humble me and encourage me to continuing to try to make the world a better place through collaborative education

WHY YOU SHOULD READ THIS BOOK

The 30 ritual of the Highly Successful People is outstanding for its brilliant ideas, original presentation, self-empowering principles, great quotes and rare gems of practical wisdom. This amazing book is truly like no other. It's more than a motivational book: it's a result-generating manual whose interactive sessions engage as well as guide you towards working out solutions to your own occupational or vision-related challenges. You'd love this life-changing book.

It's such a priceless treasure - so splendidly written with few examples drawn from the lives of pre-eminently successful people. We unreservedly recommend it to you and every person of purpose! And why not, you can send it as an unforgettable gift to someone you desire to see optimize his or her potentials.

By reading this book, you will uncover the key qualities of the highly successful people. after applying this set of qualities, you will soon find yourself living a successful life you had ever wished for.

TABLE OF CONTENTS

INTRODUCTION

When it comes down to it, no one ever said success would be easy, but if anyone did, it would be a lie. In reality, there exist no shortcuts or casual paths to succeed, no matter the value or meaning of the things you want. Yet, some people still believe they can find a loophole and get a stress-free ride.

Are you determined enough to be successful even when things are terrible? Are you someone who gives up the instant you hit a wall? Or are you the one that fights and discover an opportunity to turn that obstacle into a stepping stone to success? Are you willing to crawl just to keep moving forward?

I understand that many of us become frustrated and disappointed with the working world. As you grow up, it is an enormous disenchantment to realize that most of what you are taught by your relatives or peers about success is not the real facts.

You learn that you should just work hard at whatever job you get, and you can succeed. But when you are working hard at a position where you build someone else's dream instead of yours, or your boss does not appreciate your efforts, you are getting no satisfaction or fulfillment.

I am not trying to push you to get a business on your own but to find a better avenue for your future. If you desire to be successful, then you have to begin preparing your mind to realize that success is not going to be an easy stroll through the park.

According to the late reggae legend, Bob Marley, "Everyman thinks his burden is the heaviest". This is why people who are still struggling to succeed in life believe that the challenge of becoming a success is more difficult than whatever challenge people who have succeeded are undergoing. But on the other hands, successful people are unhappy that most unsuccessful people do not realize that there are challenges in their world. They are unhappy that others have no sympathy for the burden of challenges their achievements place on their lives.

Indeed, achieving success is an uphill task. Channeling one's effort into to the pursuit of success without accomplishing the set goal is unarguably very frustrating. Many people who are still struggling to achieve a meaningful life are convinced that achieving such goal is an uneasy task. Some of them believe that succeeding in life is the most difficult goal to accomplish. For some of them, after their consecutive efforts at achieving success continuously fail, they believe that they require the knowledge of some mysteries, not secrets, to accomplish success.

However, people who are successful consider their burden of challenge to be proportional to the heights they attain. Though becoming a success and remaining a success are challenges, the latter challenge is heavier than the former. If you watch the lives of wealthy people closely, for instance, you will observe that it is more difficult to maintain being rich than to become rich. This is also applicable to the lives of celebrities. This is why there are numerous people across the globe who failed after attaining very reputable positions in (different aspects) life.

Some people believe that they can remain at the top if anyone can assist them get there. This is very incorrect because it is more difficult to remain at the top than to get to the top. The implication of this is that if you can remain at the top if you were there, then you can get to the top. In other words, if you can remain being a success (if you were a success), then you can become a success. If it is more difficult to remain successful than to become successful, then whoever can maintain being a success can also become a success.

Do you want to be successful? If you do, in the next chapters we will talk about the 30 rituals of highly successful people that you must adopt into your life. In this book, you will discover the 30 powerful qualities that will change your life and help you to produce the results you desire.

As long as you have these qualities with you, you will be able to transform and improve the quality of your life. So are you ready to discover these 30 successful qualities? Here they are...

ALWAYS HAVE CONFIDENCE

"Believe in yourself! Have faith in your abilities! Without a humble but reasonable confidence in your own powers you cannot be successful or happy."

Norman Vincent Peale

If you have been hitting constant road blocks on your journey to success, it's quite possible that you've been trying to take short-cuts and find a easy way to the top. Like many people, you're probably at the point where you are tired of feeling like a failure and being beat up by life. All you want to do is live a life that has meaning and purpose and that satisfy your need to feel accomplished and successful. But if you lack confidence in yourself, you may have a difficult and painful road ahead of you.

Normally when you hear the term short cut to success, you usually hear of people learning from their mistakes, being placed in a position they haven't worked for, talking their way into a job they're not qualified for and things of that nature. Not often are shortcuts to success referred to when someone is trying to skip the Inner Growth Process that comes along with success.

Sometimes it feels like an impossible task to achieve the success we have desired for. I understand because I've been there!

Do You Think Confidence Equals Success?

If you said yes, you would be on the right path to your success. Confidence plays a huge role in our personal and professional lives. When we are confident and feel good about what we are doing and how we are doing it, we do more of it and that brings more success.

Take weight loss for example. I have several clients who felt a lot of doubt about whether they could get in shape and be healthy. (By the way, doubt is the antonym of confidence.) What they learned was that their success was directly related to confidence. And oh yeah, once they started to see that, boy did they get amazing results!

Don't take my word for it. Just ask 22-year-old Torey Krug a Boston Bruins defenseman who played most of the season in the minor league. Inserted into the Bruins lineup during the playoffs due to injuries, he scored two amazing goals in his first two games. He was asked by a local broadcaster what he thought attributed to his success. Torey's answer: confidence. Keep in mind this kid was no Wayne Gretzky out of college. He went undrafted. Could he have felt doubt, sure, but he didn't because he knows the road to success is paved with confidence.

If you decide to take the time out, you will begin to discover there are many great examples of confident people. While I am sure you realize there are those who have faked confidence to make them not only look good but portray a false image to the world. There are tons of examples of successful people who have achieved many great things in their lives and exude confidence with a true and real honesty.

When I talk about successful people, I do not only mean in financial and monetary terms alone. There are many ways to be a success in your life, it can be through the accumulation of knowledge, how you bring up your children, what you give to others, how you look after yourself, in regards to your health and striving to be the best that you can possibly be each and every day. To find true success in any life, then there has to be a balance in all areas of your life and when this starts to happen, your confidence rises without very much effort.

Some of the people that have been great examples of people who has great confidence are Thomas Edison, the extraordinary inventor that invented the light bulb. He never accepted failure and was confident that even though he did not succeed thousands of times, he had the confidence in his own ability that success was always within reach; Andrew Carnegie who spent half his life accumulating wealth and the second half giving it away. The confidence was in his plan and how he was going to execute it and Sir Richard Branson, who flunked out of school and had the confidence within himself that he knew he had a better plan than the education system had lined up for him.

By looking at these 3 great examples of confident people and I am sure you know there are many more, the one thing they have in common was or is their ability to achieve without any restrictions. Their ultimate strength was having the belief of their own convictions and without it, there is always going to be a doubt whether you can accomplish anything. While the examples I have given are from some extraordinary individuals, you can take heart from the fact that they were never given a silver spoon and had to work hard to get where they inevitably ended up. By working hard and having a great deal of belief in what you are doing, you will eventually reach your own heights of confidence and success.

Taking on the challenge of starting your own business takes courage; it takes an idea colliding with a dream, which creates a force of change. It takes a spark and a vision as to how you will have an impact on your target market and how your product or service will be of benefit to the world. But above all, the one thing that will ensure sustainability of your new idea and strengthen your professional relationships during negotiations with clients or customers is confidence in yourself. Confidence in the services you offer and the impact you will have on those you assist will be one of the cornerstones upon which you will build the credibility and reputation of your business.

The choice to start your own business makes a bold statement to the world around you that you believe you have the necessary skills and knowledge to contribute to the business world. But you can bet that once this statement has been made, you will be met both by those who show support and encouragement, as well as naysayers who do not have such a deep rooted belief. In other words, you will come across those who will strengthen your confidence and those who will try to undermine it. It's important to recognize what both of these perspectives serve a purpose. The positive reinforcement is just that, energy and encouragement to help you succeed. On the other hand, starting a business of your own will possess moments of nervousness and doubt, which is only natural whenever someone undertakes a project of such magnitude. The best advice would be to evaluate the feedback offered, in relation to the source from which it originates.

Overall, at the end of the day the most influential element in the process of developing and growing your business should come from the confidence you have in your own effort, energy, and abilities to bring success to your business

"Who has confidence in himself will gain the confidence of others". Looking at a successful person, we usually presume what had made the person to become so flourishing. The one and only answer to this question would be his self confidence. Without self confidence it is unattainable for a person to succeed in his life or career or whatever the affair it may be. Right from simple things to complicated things, if you need to achieve them, you need to have confidence. People with self confidence generally have excellent skills and are completely self-possessed.

Too many people overvalue what they are not, and undervalue what they are. This is the foremost blooper that everyone does. If you endeavor in building your confidence, then primarily know your talent and concentrate on things which you excel in. Find out your skills and start working on fabricating your talents. Self-confidence builds in you right from your child hood. Parental support and acceptance play a vital role in enhancing a child's confidence. Parents who encourage and support their children, each time they experience a fall are likely to build their child's self-confidence. Without self confidence nothing is possible. Hence keep in mind that, self-confidence is the primary thing that shows you the way to success.

BUILD UP YOUR PASSION

"I have no special talents. I am only passionately curious."

Albert Einstein

Do you really know what is meant by "having the passion to succeed"? The answer to this question will depend on who you ask.

Most people are married to their jobs. They don't know how to dream. They do not have any passion.

When their alarm clock shockingly awakens them from their groggy slumber with each sunrise, they grudgingly swing their feet around, get out of bed and hit the shower to wake up and prepare for the work day ahead.

They have their JOB, a.k.a. "just over broke" because they feel the need to support their family, to put sustenance on the dinner table and pay for necessities such as clothes, the electric bill, television, gas for the car, and so on.

They dream about things they "know" they can never have. That luxury sports car, a 6 bedroom home with 2 acres and a 4 car garage, a vacation home and being able to travel to exotic destinations whenever they want. Right... They are definitely not entrepreneurs!

Entrepreneurs are exceptional individuals who have an absolute passion to succeed. They know precisely what they want. Their blood starts to boil and they get excited just thinking about it!

They visualize their dreams daily. The specific goals that will get them to where they want to be are written down in detail. They have a written plan for success!

They wake up early, filled with electrical excitement, feeling their energy building for the day. They have a smile on their face before they even get out of the sack!

No, this is not a sign of mental illness! Rather it's a direct sign of mental wellness. They know what they want, have a plan, and are willing to do whatever it takes to get there (as long as it's honest and based on integrity!).

They can't wait to bolt out of bed and get to work on their dreams. They set an amazing inspirational example for everyone else.

Daily actions to get them closer to their goals and dreams are a part of the compounding baby steps took regularly.

Focus, discipline and follow through are characteristics they exhibit daily. They are in the midst of leadership transformation, of developing a leadership mindset.

You must first decide what you want in life and the direction you want to take. Having an end goal in mind is essential to achieve success. You cannot start on a journey unless you know where you are going. All the passion in the world will not do anything for you if you do not have goals and plans. Passion is the fuel for your car. Without a map, you would not be able to take your car anywhere. Making plans to achieve success is the same thing as the roadmap. Write out your long-term goals, then what you will need to do to achieve that and get started right away.

When you first start working on your long-term goals you will probably be either very excited were not too thrilled. Either way you will have to work through this stage of the process. Remember, everything is a process and you will be experiencing different emotions throughout the process. You cannot let these emotions take you off track. You must stay the course and complete your project. Use your passion to drive you towards completion, not to get distracted and check your e-mail all day long. When you develop a full force of passion, you will be unstoppable.

Make sure you channel your passion in the correct direction by using your brain. It is my opinion that passion comes from deep within. It comes from the emotional part of the brain. It is up to you to use the logical part of your brain to channel that energy in the right direction. There is something to be said about people that have a burning passion to do and accomplish their dreams in life. Many sports stars have been told they did not have the skills necessary to succeed in the professional world. Their passion is what drove them and got them there. There are many stories of people who have used their passion to achieve great success. Will you be on that list

Success takes passion and hard work. It often takes reconditioning, breaking the habits that have been subconsciously built and established over time that have gotten us to where we are... and kept us stuck there.

You must have passion in all areas of life. Passion is what creates the burning desire to make you succeed. Passion gives you the determination needed to wake up each day and continue working towards your long-term goals. Passion is what motivates you and excites you each and every day about what you do. This usually occurs when you see the potential for the work you are doing and what can be at the end of the tunnel. Use this passion as the fuel to drive you to completion of whatever project you are working on.

Focus your thoughts on those things in your life you are passionate about and success just may find you.

CREATE A POSITIVE ATTITUDE

"You cannot control what happens to you, but you can control your attitude toward what happens to you, and in that, you will be mastering change rather than allowing it to master you".

Brian Tracy

When we observe our surroundings, the environment and the people living within and around us, we learn that the world is a difficult place to live. It is not an easy task for anyone on this earth to survive and live a peaceful life. Wherever we see we find people struggling and fighting each day and each moment in order to achieve their goals and to be successful. Every human being has their set of problems and difficulties which they are trying to overcome in order to obtain what they are striving to obtain.

This constant struggle and all the obstacles that occur at every step we take become a huge cause of depression and people tend to lose heart. Then the only way to go ahead is to just keep persevering with the tasks at hand so that you could progress and finally achieve what you have set your foot out for and not leave anything half way through. At this moment, the power and force that drives us is our attitude. A positive attitude is something that makes or breaks a person. If you have a positive outlook on life, you will always look at the positive side of things.

Looking for the positives in everything you do and see will ensure that you are content and happy and live a life full of optimism and hope. Hope is of course what we all live by as no one knows what GOD has kept in store for us. Therefore, there is absolutely no use being negative and spreading the negativity around. By doing this we will not only damage ourselves but also damage our surroundings and the people we are related to in some way or the other.

Thomas Jefferson says:

"Nothing can stop the man with the right mental attitude from achieving his goal; nothing on earth can help the man with the wrong mental attitude."

It is actually all about our mindset. If we decide that everything is good and look for the positives, we will find that things are actually great. Similarly, if we want to see all negative, then we would find negatives and discrepancies in even the positive things in life. Hence, it is important to keep a positive mindset and outlook on life.

Kahlil Gibran says:

"Your living is determined not so much by what life brings to you as by the attitude you bring to life; not so much by what happens to you as by the way your mind looks at what happens".

What needs to be done has to be done. We can either choose to do it with an unthankful and ungrateful attitude or we can do it with a smile on our face, but we have to do it in either case.

Therefore, the obviously right way to go solve the issue is to do it in a positive light and with the hope that this hard time will pass and everything will be sorted out eventually. We just need to be patient, wait for the right time and believe in our GOD.

We cannot control others and we cannot change others. The only thing that we can control and change is our attitude. Once we alter our own attitude, the world all of a sudden looks a rosy place and everything seems to fall into place.

As human beings, we need to learn to be thankful and happy in all situations. No matter what the circumstances, we should always give it our best shot and should try to see things in a positive light. Positivity literally takes all the unhappiness, pain and negativity away from our life. We always have a choice. There is nothing in this world that happens to us without our will and desire. If we feel good, it is because we chose to feel good and if we feel bad, it is because that's the way we want to feel.

Similarly, attitude is a choice that we need to make. We can choose to alter our attitude towards positivity or negativity and all that happens to us is because of us only. We cannot blame anyone else for the way we feel and the way we see the world. All that really matters is the fact that we give it our best shot and should not have any regrets.

So please, keep a positive attitude on life, work hard towards your goals and keep the positive attitude going under all circumstances. Eventually, we will all reach our destination and achieve our desired goals and the world will be a much better place.

CULTIVATE HIGH SELF ESTEEM

"Love yourself first and everything else falls into line. You really have to love yourself to get anything done in this world."

Lucille Ball

What is Self-esteem? Where do we get it from? Why it is so important in life? As child we had very high self esteem. But, as we grow up between two to nine years old we start losing it due to the influence by others like parents, teachers, friends, preacher and leaders etc. We begin to push down our self. Most of youngster loss ether self-esteem by the time they leave high school.

What we need to do is to re-discover our self- esteem and take 100% responsibility of life. No one else is responsible for our self-esteem. Underneath each of us, we have enough strength to be where you want to be. In order to be a confident person we should have build up more knowledge and feel more comfortable to meet different situations in life. So that you should be able to take more risk and participate more in life.

In order to learn and be successful you have to take action and risk. The more problems and difficult situation we face in life in fact make us stronger. If you feel some kind of belongings your self-esteem will go high. So it is recommended you to be the part of some kind of groups where you feel lovable. You may share all your vision, mission or you short-term and long-term goal with your group so that your group members can help you to achieve it.

Relationship or social contact is very important to keeping yourself as part of a community. Be part of a community service volunteers. Attend seminars and workshop where you can meet lot of similar kind people.

Ability to respond to the events is our power. You cannot control all events but you can control the way you respond to that. Based on your response to the events each time it produces the outcome differently. You can make wonders by changing your response to the events.

Believe in yourself. No one can bring your self-esteem down by saying or acting negative to you. No one can make you inferior or upset without your consent. You start telling yourself after they stop talking to you. Those self talks determine how your self-esteem goes.

Accept and appreciate what you do and your appearance. You need to focus five aspect of your personality to keep your self-esteem high. They are your mind, imaginations, body, emotions and Spiritual self.

In the mind you should have a positive thought, affirmations, positive self talks, and believes. In the imagination, you should have to create positive image, pictures and positive visualization about events. You must accept your body as it is and learn to love your body. Appreciate the function it doing. Accept your body even though it is overweight. Stop producing negative emotions like guilt and resemble. Keep in touch with yourself and realize the ultimate purpose of this life. Spend some time everyday and sit in a quiet place and meditate. Plan your day from there.

Always remember that no matter what other person say or do to you, you are a worthwhile person. Replace the negative thought by a positive one. You will find yourself with high self-esteem and your success in every area follows you.

MAKE A CLEAR VISION

"If you get the inside right, the outside will fall into place"

Eckhart Tolle

Most people will think about this statement and refer to something about their personal well-being; their inner talk creating their outer reality. It's interesting how the conversations in our minds dictate our behavior and furthermore; our results, favorable or not.

If you embrace this statement, you will become more aware of how important it is to get the inside right. And a part of getting the outside to fall into place in relationship to the inside is knowing what you want it to look and feel like.

What about your business? Do you have a vision for it? Most of us have a pretty good idea that we want success in our businesses. We can SEE the final product of the fruits of our labor. We may even be able to easily envision ourselves sitting on the beach outside the incredible home that we will enjoy in the future when we achieve and accomplish our goals and dream; then sit back to enjoy a early retirement while the business we built sustains us and our families.

But how can we achieve this?

We can do this by creating a compelling vision that is in alignment with our inner values. Once we are completely clear about our vision and our values we will be able to attract the means to achieve the success we desire. Without a vision, we are forced to live our lives by simply reacting to the circumstances that happen to come our way. We may even be able to "make the best of them" and "manage to make ends meet" but if there's no vision then we may never have any idea where we are going. We have no LIGHT shining towards the ultimate goal ahead of us. We find ourselves sitting in a dream car but without the KEY we can't drive it anywhere. A MASTER of success creates opportunities that align with their core values and then uses them to transform what they see in front of them into opportunities that will lead them to the results they are seeking.

Change is a fact of life.

Nothing ever stays the same.

The proof of this lies in our mirrors every day. But most people spend their lives fighting to keep what they know and are comfortable with the same in spite of the fact that deep down inside they feel dissatisfaction or disconnection. Yet, they are sure that the harder they try to hold on to what's familiar, the better they will ultimately feel. In fact, they may even be expecting positive changes in their lives by subconsciously hanging on to familiar habits and strategies while expecting different results. Someone called this the definition of insanity but it's actually just a common survival means that ALL of us has used at one time or another. But these habits are not proactive nor they able to drive us towards success. Success cannot be forced without creating tremendous stress that drains our resources and our souls.

The key to remember about success is that it is not a desire. It is not even a goal. Success is a result. It is the "after" of your "before."

In order to be successful we must be able to work smarter, not harder. We must have a clear understanding of our core values and how they align with our business goals. Our dreams and goals are simply waiting for us to step into them. And, unfortunately, they will continue to wait until we take the steps necessary to put them exactly where they belong.

KEEP READING

"Reading maketh a full man; conference a ready man; and writing an exact man. "

Francis Bacon

It is not a secret that reading is the key to success; we have been told and taught this from a very early age. Remember all those book reports you had to do for free pizza in elementary school? And now in the age of the internet—reading, writing, and communication skills are more valuable than any other skills you possess. What is the key to great communication and writing skills? You guessed it, reading.

Reading is an important part of our society. It is key to learning and understanding. Without reading, how would you know where to buy that juicy hamburger on the billboard? Or what would happen if Christian Bale couldn't read his script for the new Batman movie? Well, he probably wouldn't sound that different, but you get the point. Reading is a key factor to life as we know it.

In my study of successful people, the one thing they all seem to have in common is a passion and dedication for reading. Below is an example from warren buffet and Charlie monger

Warren Buffett and Charlie Munger

I group these two together because of the extent to which they share the same ideologies. The duo is legendary for their longstanding business and investing prowess through investments at Berkshire Hathaway, which has consistently outperformed the market since its inception.

The result has spawned an army of devoted followers and has earned Buffett and Munger titles of two of the richest men on the planet. As a testament to their influence, thousands of people fly in from across the world to spend just a day listening to Buffett and Munger speak at their annual shareholder's meeting.

So when Buffett or Munger give advice, we should listen. The two largely share the same philosophies on best business practices and investment styles, and they also happen to agree on the same method for success. In a 2007 commencement speech given at the USC School of Law, Charlie Munger said: I constantly see people rise in life who are not the smartest, sometimes not even the most diligent, but they are learning machines. They go to bed every night a little wiser than they were when they got up and boy does that help, particularly when you have a long run ahead of you.

He goes on to reference Buffett as an example of such a learning machine:

If you watched Warren Buffett with a time clock, I would say half of all the time he spends is just sitting on his ass and reading. And a big chunk of the rest of the time is spent talking on the phone or personally with people he trusts.

Buffett echoes his partner's sentiments. When asked how to get smarter at a conference, he held up a stack of papers and said:

Read 500 pages like this every day. That's how knowledge works. It builds up, like compound interest. All of you can do it, but I guarantee not many of you will.

These successful people worked or continue to work in a range of fields spanning business, investing, technology, politics, public speaking, civil rights and leadership.

They lived or live through different periods of time with different purposes and missions in life. Yet the common link among them is their affinity for reading and their accreditation of success to that key trait.

The takeaway is, regardless of your endeavor, your current situation, your upbringing, or the path you wish to take in life, reading is the key to upward mobility. It may not guarantee success, but it surely increases the chances of it.

Fortunately, the amount of time we spend reading is entirely within our control, so get to it.

ADMIT YOUR MISTAKES

"A person, who never made a mistake, never tried anything new. "

Albert Einstein

Growing teaches you a lot of important lessons about life and I can say that I have definitely learned a lot during the course of 21 years.

The important lessons I learned were to treat others with respect and how to deal with the treatment from others. Every person is different and they are not going to always do things, the way you would like things to happen.

From experience there have been a lot of people and moments that have let me down. So many that I started to take that anger and frustration out on people who had nothing to do with the person that caused my attitude to change. When I took that frustration and anger out on others, it only drew them away and I may not have known but they probably questioned my character as well. Believe it or not I was not always this boy who can't trust, with an attitude and chose to be distant from others because of the fear that trusting in someone for once would back fire. I used to be this really kind, sweet, loyal, happy, friendly person but when I was that age people took my kindness for weakness.

Therefore, I had to grow some backbone but now I realize I might have grown a little too much and cut people out of my life that deserved it. Maybe I was looking for all the wrong things in a person which is not good because those type of traits never usually follow through with anything and are not loyal. So this summer I've managed to take a deeper look at myself, in and out. During this process, I grew to really love and appreciate myself as a whole (body, mind, and soul).

People naturally avoid what they fear. Unfortunately, people are often afraid of the very activities necessary to their success. Success requires failure few time; success requires foolish mistakes and years of learning. If you want to succeed, you need to get comfortable with failure, foolishness, and ignorance. Here are some thoughts that might help:

BEING WILLING TO FAIL CAN LEAD TO SUCCESS.

Do you remember Babe Ruth? During his life, he was known as the "homerun" king. But did you know that he also held the record for strikeouts? Did you know that Edison's light bulb experiment failed 10,000 times before he got the thing to work? And how long did it take you to perfect walking, reading, or speaking? Don't be afraid to fail. Failure is a necessary part of the learning process. Lincoln bankrupted two businesses and was defeated in several elections before becoming President. Does that make him a failure, or a success?

Emerson once wrote;

"Whatever you do, you need courage. Whatever course you decide upon, there will always be someone to tell you, you are wrong. There are always difficulties arising, which tempt you to believe that your critics are right."

People will always be quick to point out your failures, and you're bound to have a few. So you might as well get comfortable with people noticing. Once you've gotten comfortable with being wrong occasionally, you might actually discover how to get things right.

DON'T BE AFRAID TO LOOK STUPID:

No matter how much you try to avoid it, you will probably look stupid at least once in your life. So instead of dreading that moment's arrival, you might as well get it over with. Just go ahead and do something that looks stupid. Join an acting class, and try to be awful. Go to a karaoke bar, and sing off key on purpose.

You'll discover that nobody really cares if you look stupid. People are too busy trying to hide their own stupidity to remember yours, and anyone with an opinion that matters is certainly not keeping a record on you. Besides, once you are comfortable looking stupid, you won't have to fear it so much.

WE ARE ALL BORN IGNORANT AND LACKING IN EXPERIENCE.

A lot of people seem to believe that ignorance means the same as stupid. They don't want to admit when they don't know something because they fear appearing dumb.

Ignorance does not mean stupid. Ignorance simply means that we lack information, training and experience. We are all ignorant of many things, just as we are all knowledgeable of many things. After all, we're all born ignorant of life. So why do people feel threatened when they have to admit that they don't know something? Stop trying to hide your ignorance; instead, proclaim it proudly. Whenever you pretend that you know everything, or actually think that you know everything, you short-circuit your only path towards growth.

I think it is very important to really learn to appreciate and love yourself during the course of your life because it makes life much more understandable and you appreciate everything that you have. Before I used to speak it but not actually look at myself and sometimes admit, I make mistakes and I am Sorry! I am sorry for giving up. I am sorry for taking my pain out on others. I am sorry for feeling sorry for myself and not believing that there is a bigger purpose for life. I appreciate me and my life. I just pray for better days and much success to come.

DEVELOP SELF- DISCIPLINE

"With self-discipline most anything is possible."

Theodore Roosevelt

Imagine getting to the stage that you do the tough things in life on auto pilot. How wonderful would that be? It takes perseverance to get to that stage. The mind does some strange things that has an impact on our decision- making process. The Sandler Sales System calls all this negative stuff floating around in our minds "Head Trash". How true is that? The self-improvement industry is chalk full of books, Cd's and online support websites of some of the biggest names in the business. All this support is directed at a never ending supply of people who want to make an improvement in their lives. Heck, I have been a supporter of the business for many years. I love it to the point that I now write about my experiences and things that I have learned along the way. As successful as I have become I still keep

Searching for ways to make myself better. So what does all this have to do with self discipline? Everything.

To have self discipline does not mean that you are a boring person. It does not mean that you have your life planned minute by minute. To the contrary. When you have self discipline you have a tendency to get the hard stuff done first. This affords you the time to be spontaneous. More importantly you will make decisions on what you do in your free time based on your over all goals. I believe this to be true.

So how do we achieve or improve our self discipline? Here are some tips that have worked for me.

The first step is to write down a few goals that emotionally charge you. I believe when you have goals that will make you feel good, the emotional attachment will drive you to succeed. Success is imminent when you are passionate about what you want.

The second step is to enter in your diary when you are going to work toward these goals. Yes. Make an appointment with yourself. This will give you a reason to say no when something else comes along. You simply say I am working on a project right now that needs my attention. Just imagine how liberating it is when you have a commitment this strong. Success is now in your grasp.

The third step is to find an accountability partner. This will take some effort on your behalf but it will be the reinforcement of steps one and two. An accountability partner is someone who you share your goals with. I personally have one. We have an appointment at the same time each week and we discuss our progress toward our goals. So how do you feel about telling your accountability partner that you did not

Work towards your goal this week. Exactly. It feels awful. I have learned from experience that having the right person as an accountability partner is key. Someone who is simply a cheerleader will not do. Your accountability partner must also have realistic goals. Both of you have important things at stake. It works.

The success and "big wins" we all so deeply want to experience in our business comes with discipline. It's clearly knowing what you want and then taking consistent action each and every day to make that happen. With discipline comes order and with order comes success!

Self discipline will bring control into your decision-making process. Self discipline will remove some of the second guessing we are all guilty of. Self discipline will help you focus on what you want to accomplish. Being in control of our emotions and working toward what makes us happy is a good thing for all of us. The work can be fun too when the end result will bring you so much happiness and joy.

BE FLEXIBLE

"it is not the strongest or the most intelligent who will survive, but those who can best manage change"

Leon C. Megginson

you will get more of the success you seek, as soon as you learn to be more flexible! Flexibility in all areas of life can help you achieve success and help you inspire others to find their own version of success, as well.

Every day the world changes, you should be flexible in life because nothing remains the same. It's important that you don't allow yourself to be left behind while you're still exactly the same.

To get success, you should always be flexible. Try new things if your old ways of doing them is not giving any results. You must never get too rigid in your thinking, actions, or even your beliefs. You'll be hurting yourself if you don't want to change in life. Everybody is capable of changing therefore you should be flexible with the changing times.

Even if you don't agree with everything that's happening around you, you should be able to move along with it. You should be flexible, don't go against the changing world because you'll definitely lose. It's better to embrace change, and continue to grow and develop personally.

As the world changes, it doesn't mean that you can't stand up for what you think is right, you should also be willing to accept the things that you can never have control of. It's better for you to face the challenges and never permit yourself to just sit about complaining, when you may well be working hard to achieve your goals.

If you've ever had that feeling of standing on shifting sand, you'll know how we're feeling. Plans are ripping themselves out of the pad and flying out of the window.

I guess there are many people who will empathies and think that it's pointless making plans and having goals when other people's actions can mean they have to be redrawn. Why bother!

Well, I think it's only by having goals that you will have some order in your life when everything around you is changing. It does mean however that you might have to tweak them, but measuring success, reviewing and making changes to your goals are all part of the process.

It might be better for you to have daily goals which may be easier to achieve. For example you could say that by the end of the day you will have rung 10 people, decluttered your office, spent an hour tackling some of your mounting paperwork and picked up your dry cleaning.

Maybe these could turn into weekly goals, so that by the end of the week you would have contacted a number of people, finished decluttering your office, got your paperwork in order and tackled some of your domestic chores such as setting up internet shopping.

If that works, try monthly goals next, but be prepared to be flexible. Set the goal, set a measure of success, review and be prepared to tweak along the way.

We can't predict everything in our lives but it seems to me that rolling with the changes and being prepared to review and modify your goals can still help you to feel you're in control.

one of the problems most of us run into is that if one thing is working well, we then choose to change six things simultaneously. it is a trap!!

a much better, saner, and more sustainable strategy is to take small steps to get to where you need to go. everyone comes with a different skill set. you may be a flexible person who just needs to expand, or you may need to work on gaining flexibility as a whole. you cannot expect to become a different person overnight, but with small steps you will indeed be there soon.

PATIENCE IS A VIRTUE

"Patience, persistence and perspiration make an unbeatable combination for success. "

Napoleon Hill

Once people learn to walk and talk, if able to do so without difficulty, they seem to forget that it took time and patience to succeed at these very complex tasks. There were more times of misspoken words or tumbles on the floor than could be counted. Parents often smiled or laughed at the imperfect attempts to learn these skills now performed with little or no thought.

Success Takes Patience

Whenever you attempt to learn something new, you have to give yourself time to acquire the fundamentals of your soon to be new skill. There is a complex interaction and imprinting occurring in the brain. New neural pathways are being traced every time you try something new. As you practice it, the neural pathways strengthen.

Nature, not technology, is the metaphor for time and success. A healthy human baby takes a full nine months. You might be able to get by with 8.5 months, but every parent worries when a baby comes much earlier than that.

As wonderful as technology is, its instant gratification model gives the false impression that you can accomplish great things in moments. Yes, it takes much less time to edit a book you've put in your computer, but it still involves butt-time in the chair with fingers hitting the keyboard to have anything worth editing.

From Idea to Completion

Think of your idea as a seed and your mind, from which your idea came, as the fertile soil it will grow in. Your idea needs time to incubate. Once you acknowledge it by bringing it into your conscious mind and affirm it by saying, "Yes, I want this to happen," your unconscious mind begins to allow the idea to grow roots and a stem.

You feed and water your idea by giving it time, sketching out plans, gathering information and talking about it with mentors. Your idea continues to grow as you itemize the objectives that will move you on the road to success. Once you have the information and learning you need to get started, you take the first step on the journey. Your seed has pushed through the top of the soil.

Success Includes Mishaps

Just as you fell often on your diapered bottom when you learned to walk, you will fall on your road to accomplishing your goals. You will try certain strategies and some will work and others won't. The key is to have patience with the process. When a strategy doesn't work out, that simply means you have gathered information about what not to do. You come up with additional options and try those.

The only failure is quitting. Ask Thomas Edison, the inventor of the incandescent light bulb. He tried more than 1000 different elements for the filament in the light bulb. Time and patience is what moved society from oil lamps to electric lamps.

THINK BIG, DREAM BIG, MAKE IT HAPPEN

"No matter where you're from, your dreams are valid."

Lupita Nyong'o

Many people remain largely poor and financial dwarfs and unsuccessful because of their limited capacity to dream. They either have small dreams or no dreams at all. Limited dreams lead to limited success because you cannot hit where you have not targeted. When you have no dream, you can be taken anywhere and by anybody.

In order to achieve big things in your life, you must be willing to think big. You should dream big and envision your goals to make them happen. Achieving your targets and goals is best achieved when you can imagine every detail of what it is you want to achieve.

When you're busily working toward bringing your goals to life, you also feel happier and more fulfilled in your journey.

Follow these steps to bring your goals to fruition by envisioning what you want in life:

Close your eyes and imagine your future.

Where do you see yourself in a year, five years or ten? Try to think as far ahead as you comfortably can. Do you see yourself with a family, children, a steady job, and a college degree in ten years?

Try to have as vivid a visualization as you can. Pay attention to every detail, and let your dreams come to life in your mind, showing you what matters most to you. Think about where you want to be in the future and how you want to get there.

Write down everything you envision.

Use as much detail as you can when jotting down what you remember. Write down the most important achievements that you focused on, but also the details about each. What matters most to you?

Note the things that stood out in your visualization. Did you own your own home? Were you raising a family? Did you have a job that made you happy? Were you making a comfortable income? What other details stood out? How did you feel.

Create a list of bullet points.

Do this for each separate achievement that you wrote about following your visualization. For example, if one of your achievements is "I own my own home," then you can list things like you are successfully saving for a down payment, that you're making monthly mortgage payments, and you have a steady job.

Break each of these bullet points down into goals.

For example, if one bullet point was to save for a down payment for the home you visualized, how can you get there? Create savings goals that will allow you to work toward having a down payment for your home.

Lay out your plan.

Once you have a list of long term, medium term, and short term goals in mind, create a plan accordingly. How will you achieve these goals? How will you bring the life that you visualized into existence? Divide your large goals into achievable steps

Start achieving goals today.

Put your future plans into action today. try to take a small step each day toward the future you have envisioned. Move forward every day, even if you are only taking small steps at a time.

Revisit your plan consistently.

Visualizations, dreams, and hopes change over time. Revisit the plan that you laid out and the future goals that you dreamed up on a consistent basis to ensure their relevancy over time. It's okay to change your dreams and goals based on your needs and desires as they change.

Visualizing the "dream you" is an excellent way to bring your goals to the forefront when you're trying to determine what matters most to you.

When you can picture what your desired life is like, you can better determine the goals you need to set and achieve to get there. All it takes are small steps toward your desired future self, and you can achieve the life you deserve!

WORK ON YOUR CREATIVITY

"Creative thinking inspires ideas. Ideas inspire change."

Barbara Januszkiewicz

We are all creative beings and we are designed for expansion and fuller expression. There is no other basic principle of life than this truth. We always want to be better, we always want to have more and do more; that is human nature and nature as we know it. It is our spiritual purpose, to create or co-create. We are the creators of our own reality. No one on this planet can righteously say that they are not creative. It is something that we are born with and we take with us to the day that we pass.

We are constant creators and we never stop creating our realities. Look at our technology, the internet, our homes, our communications, our clothes, our food, furniture and fixtures. How can anyone dare say they are not creative? We take ideas from nowhere and make them something that people want or need. We learn to fix things, take initiative in the office, raise children and even more. We write, sing, dance, play musical instruments, paint and build highways.

It is our nature to be creative. You can deny this or simply accept it as truth. The fact remains that we are creators of our own realities. Some people may not be creative artist, but may be creative engineers, just because we use the rules that fit our professions doesn't make us any less creative than the next guy.

I will give you an example. Just look at Michael Jordan who's both talented and creative. But even Michael Jordan was cut from his high school team! Do you get where I'm going here?

The point is Michael Jordan wasn't always as talented or creative as we came to know him, but he did possess a desire to develop himself to the greatest ability he could imagine. Ah, desire & imagination, two of the most delicious words in the English language. Part of the magic beneath creativity and talent are desire and imagination. It's this tag team duo that will send you down the path of no return in pursuit of nurturing your creative and talent wellspring.

Remember that capacity lies within us all. You too can achieve high levels of greatness and achievement through honestly developing your talents and creativity. From there, as they say, the sky is the limit; and if you don't believe me, than just look at Michael Jordan!

To be successful in any given course of activity, one at times must be innovative or creative in some fashion. We don't always have the right circumstances or the right resources at hand to do

anything. We are forced by nature and Universal Law to be creative. There is no denying that when presented with a problem that one of our most major resources and capabilities is our own natural creativity.

BE AN ENTHUSIASTIC

"Success consists of going from failure to failure without loss of enthusiasm. "

Winston Churchill

Enthusiasm is one of the most powerful forces in the universe. It is the force that often makes the difference between the mediocre and the superstars. In every field of human endeavor; be it sports or politics, business or the arts; nobody has ever made it to the top without a healthy dose of enthusiasm. In fact in the history of the world nothing great has ever been achieved without enthusiasm.

We all know that enthusiasm produces success. So why write more about it? Because, often, we are more enthusiastic about what we don't want than what we want. Take a typical office during lunch break. What conversations do you most hear? The loudest, and most enthusiastic, are usually over all the things people don't want to happen. Complaints about the boss, complaints about customers, the size of the paycheck, the bad weather, who just betrayed who, who has the worst job, the worst car, the worst home. We are a society that complains enthusiastically! Now enters a person who has just accomplished a major task successfully. As he begins to describe what he did that was successful, with enthusiasm, eyes roll and heads turn. Comments like - "He's bragging again." OR "There he goes trying to show everyone off" are heard. Somehow it's become OK to be enthusiastic about our failures, and not OK to be enthusiastic about our successes.

This comes from the mis-use of energy in the third chakra, the solar plexus area of personal power. Our "gut feelings" have been permitted to be expressed only in their negative mode of judgment and jealously. Instead of wanting to be around successful people so we, too, may catch the energy of success, we feel more comfortable being around those who are less successful than we are. The former makes us feel inferior, while the later makes us feel superior. But enthusiasm and success are not about being better than, or worse than, anyone else. They are about discovering our own unique passions in life, and enthusiastically fulfilling them to reach phenomenal goals.

To develop the enthusiasm for success begins by becoming enthusiastic about the little things in your life. What if you woke up every morning saying "Wow - this is great, I'm here!" To find that energy, just look at how a puppy wakes up. Wag your tail at the day! Then, during the day, express enthusiasm over every little thing. Shout out loud things like "Wow, my car started up when I turned the key!" and "Look at that beautiful morning sun!" and "I really packed a great lunch for myself today!". Keep being enthusiastic all day long! It's harder than it sounds. We are use to going quietly through our days, energetically shouting about the negative, and quietly accepting the positive. It's something about not being "prideful" that has developed as our unwritten rule. But, just watch Donald Trump on TV. He's enthusiastic about his successes. And many think of him as egotistic. He may be, or not, I don't know because I haven't met him. I do know that he is successful and that he appears to really enjoy his success enthusiastically.

Many people I know are filled with Light but hide it because they don't want to appear egotistic. And they lose opportunities for success. You can't give what you don't have. If you are not successful monetarily, then you can't give money to worthy causes and charities. If you are not successful professionally, than you can't share your knowledge and wisdom with others. If you are not successful in loving yourself, then you can't feel and express love for others. Whatever your goal, whatever means success to you, generate enthusiasm and let the energy carry you to your dream. It really doesn't matter what other people may say about you. All that matters is your own excitement about your coming success. Dare to succeed. And dare to be enthusiastic. And remember, practice makes perfect!

POSSESS A GOOD CHARACTER

"Character is destiny."

Unknown

There is a direct relationship between character and success, in that you cannot have one without the other. In fact, your success is defined by your character.

We live in a society today where success has become an arbitrary accomplishment. Any online personality with enough followers on Twitter, any entrepreneur who reaches a million dollars in sales, or any politician not caught with his pants around his ankles is considered successful. In reality, there should be (and for many people, continues to be) a higher standard of success.

Good character is something that should not be just for show when you are in front of other people. In fact, one's true character manifests most especially when you are acting by yourself or when you think no one else is looking.

Character is something that is intrinsically within a person and is above race, religion, age or gender, and even education and one's personality. Character traits will determine how a person responds or reacts when faced with a certain situation in life.

For example, if someone has honesty as a character trait, he will always be truthful and say things that are true as opposed to a person who is not honest. Many successful people are known to have strong and good character, and they consider this as their basic foundation. Many people can have riches and resources, but if one does not know what is good character and does not apply it in their lives, then they will never know what it means to be truly successful.

There are six attributes which can be called to form the pillars of a GOOD CHARACTER. These are:

• Trustworthiness;

• Respect;

• Responsibility;

• Fairness;

• Caring and

• Citizenship

Good character has benefits more than one. It brings to our soul immense happiness, satisfaction and a feeling of living a complete and ideal life. It attracts the trust and respect of other people, besides allowing us to influence others. It changes our perspective about failure, sustains us through difficult times or opposition. It builds our self esteem, self respect and confidence stronger. The list doesn't end here. It also creates a foundation for happy, healthy relationships. It keeps us committed to our values and goals. Ultimately, it improves the chances of our success in work and other endeavors.

To build good character traits:

• Define your core values

• Practice the habits which are morally sound

• Find people with character

• Commit to self-improvement

• Take some risks towards your goal

So, now it's entirely in your hand to attract the best things in the world towards yourself by bettering your own character and leading an exemplary life full of achievements and good deeds!

BE DETERMINED

"A dream doesn't become reality through magic; it takes sweat, determination and hard work."

Colin Powell

An insight into the system of creation reveals that... Every being, you and I inclusive, that comes into existence develops and grows in struggle and adversity... right from the first day of its life until when it hits the highest point of perfection. It's a well established norm of nature that rules... over all.

Every person is thus inclined to select the shortest path to success and to get result from its effort as soon as possible. This is the way we are...all, ABSOLUTELY. Well, as you and I know...In any kind of undertaking, one cannot shorten his path to success without...patience, persistence and determination and reach the desired objective. There is NO possibility of progress and/or success without this moral virtue. To quote Calvin Coolidge:

"Nothing in this world can take the place of persistence. Talent will not; nothing is more common than unsuccessful people with talent. Genius will not; unrewarded genius is almost a proverb. Persistence and determination alone are omnipotent. The slogan "press on" has solved and always will solve the problems of the human race."

Anyone who desires to achieve success in any undertaking, whether he is a man of ordinary talents or someone endowed with exceptional creativity, will power, intelligence and genius... must cultivate persistence and determination.

Else...

A great task is NEVER accomplished instantaneously and spontaneously. Rather... An enormous amount of ENERGY, in any of its form, and TIME is required to bring them to fruition. While there are some who languish behind the caravan of life, you'll observe some others achieve remarkable success.

The basic difference between these two sets of people lies in the QUALITY of their efforts and the EXTENT of their steadfastness, persistence and determination. Think of anything at all...? WHY WAIT. Your success is determined by YOU and ONLY you. Be patient, persistent, and determined... Success is SURE to come.

IMPROVE YOUR COMMUNICATION SKILL

"Communication - the human connection - is the key to personal and career success."

Paul J. Meyer

Improve your communication skill and you can slowly work your way towards success. In today's world of information, it is essential to improve your communication skill in order to move forward and prosper.

Being able to effectively communicate with others means that you have the capability to receive and relay information, a very important asset considering that information today has become a valued asset.

Being able to communicate effectively means more than just being articulate. Many other factors are required for effective communication. You have to know them in order for you to improve your communication skill. They also rely on having a keen ear aside from having a way with the spoken word. Here are some tips that will be able to help you improve your communication skill.

Effective communication relies on your ability to listen. Being an attentive listener allows you to gather all the information that you can get from a certain conversation. Being an attentive listener also means that you focus on what is being said and make sure that you comprehend the point.

A good way to improve on your comprehension is by learning to get involved in the conversation. Know how to ask questions whenever you think you miss out on a certain point. Try to make use of your other senses during an ongoing conversation. The more you involve your other senses, the more you would stay interested on what is being said.

During conversations, try to respond instead of trying to react. Responding entails the use of your mind before you speak whereas reacting usually involves your emotion. Responding always keeps you in control as you mindfully oversee what you wish to say. Reacting, on the other hand, can let a conversation get out of hand, which is not the aim of effective communication.

The most important tip that you need to do to improve your communication skill is constant practice. Try to participate in as many discussions and social interactions as you can. Try to practice the art of listening as well as contributing to the conversation. As you go along, you will notice a considerable improvement on them. If there is a lack of possible discussions to participate in, you can always practice on your own friends and family. After all, effective communication can be used in different aspects of your life, be it at work at play. Always remember that effective communication is a way of building relationships.

As you strive to improve your communication skill, you will eventually find success along the way.

ALWAYS BE PREPARED

"Before anything else, preparation is the key to success."

Alexander Graham Bell

It is beyond mortal discretion to fathom how much can be achieved by executing a task after proper prior preparation. It is surprising how the average people do not value the importance of preparation in life. They allow themselves to perform important tasks without adequate preparation. Executing a task without ample preparation is a recipe for failure.

Anyone can desire to be successful, but it takes preparation to really succeed in life.

A lawyer who stands before the jury unprepared can cost a client millions of dollars in a lawsuit. A student who sits for an examination without proper prior preparation or planning only has his or her own ineptitude to blame for second-rate results. A business executive meeting shareholders without preparing for the same only stand to invoke the scorn of the shareholders. In every field of endeavour; social, political, economical and spiritual, preparation is the bright golden thread woven through every comportment of success.

In a business negotiation the prospect can tell if the negotiator is unprepared. In an interview the interviewer does not need exceptional perception to conclude whether the interviewee is prepared or not. Unpreparedness can cause irreparable damage to your reputation and professionalism. It is unequivocally advisable not to perform a task for which you are unprepared.

When tackling any kind of job, if you invest sufficient time in preparation, a relatively small amount of effort and time will be required for carrying out. Conversely if preparation is not thought through, application of more effort and mediocre results can become inevitable. It is astonishing how most people just go ahead and execute without proper prior preparation. Try to recall how frustrating it was the last time that you attempted to do a job or make a sales presentation for which you were unprepared. Remember those sneering looks and brusque retorts, let alone the stammering. You can spare yourself such ridicule by carefully taking time to prepare. Preparation brings with it extraordinarily impressive results. Proper preparation propels you to greater heights.

When you get yourself prepared for any encounter, it could be a job interview, a marketing presentation or an examination, the sense of massive confidence and psychological edge that you gain enables you to perform at your best. When you take time to study your customer, getting to understand what they want and why they want it that way, your figures will quadruple and you will certainly leave your competitors in the dust. Analyze the trends in your industry. Figure out why some commodities are falling in price while others are rising. Look at the figures, analyze your competition. Understand the needs of your customer. Polish the words that you will use in front of the prospect and avoid the temptation of saying the wrong words at inappropriate times. Break through the barrier that causes preparation time to be labeled "unproductive time."

Preparation separates the winners from the also-rans. When Toyota wanted to venture into manufacturing of luxury vehicles for the US market, its research team was sent to live luxuriously and learn the tastes and preferences of its prospective customers. They lived in Laguna Beach, California for several months just to get an appreciation of what their customers wanted. US$1billion was invested in the project and out of this a powerful LS400 was born. Needless to say, the venture was a considerable success. If you develop the habit of preparing for any task at hand you are guaranteed to swim upstream all your life.

It is as certain as night follows day that if you continue living on the planet you will complete the next ten years. The question is what plans have you put in place for those ten years? What have you planned for your life in the next twenty, thirty and fifty years? The prudent break them into smaller periods and assess their progress gradually. This helps to determine whether you are progressing towards your goals or drifting thereby allowing for the necessary adjustments to be made. If you do not plan for your life you will still live but the question is how? What kind of a lifestyle will you lead? This is the period that many people are finalizing or have already finalized their new year's plans or resolutions. Instead of focusing solely on 2017 I would urge you to broaden your horizon and stretch yourself further to the next five, ten and twenty years. When the time progresses as it will surely do you will be found prepared for what life has to offer.

Some say that luck is nothing other than chance meeting preparedness. No matter who you are or where you come from, if you invest sufficient time in preparing for what you have to do excellently you will develop a self-propelled upward spiral. Do not rush to implement before you are certain that enough time and resources have been put into preparation. Take time to get yourself prepared for who you want to be in the future. You do not have to wait for the future to come before you start preparing. Start preparing now and the future will find you prepared.

ALWAYS BE COMMITTED

"Individual commitment to a group effort - that is what makes a team work, a company work, a society work, a civilization work."

Vince Lombardi

OK, so you've taken time to dream. You've started exploring your passion. You've even begun to set goals for yourself. Now it's time to take seriously your efforts to succeed.

Success takes commitment. Success takes time. To experience success in any area of your life, you have to be able to push past life's road blocks. Commit to not quit! Focus your thoughts on the prize you seek, not the challenges. One of my favorite remedies for the tough times is saying aloud, "I will not be defeated and I will not quit." Repeat as needed.

Commitment requires discipline. If you've made a commitment - to yourself or someone else, use discipline to fulfill that promise. Not only will it help you reach your goals, you'll feel better about yourself in the process.

The quality of a person's life is in direct proportion to their commitment to excellence, regardless of their chosen field of endeavor. - Vince Lombardi

Commitment is aided by routine. Commit to spending a certain amount of time each day on your goal or to focus on the project at a specific time each day. Use your most creative time of day to work on your greatest challenges. For some, that's early morning, before the day's events interfere. Some are most creative and energetic in the afternoon. Others prefer the quiet of evening. Whatever works for you, if you'll make it a routine, it will soon become a habit. The habit of commitment will carry you to success.

Commitment requires tough decisions. I've always told my friend, "If you spend it there, you won't have it to spend somewhere else". The same is true with your time, talents, energy. Use your internal check list (peace) to decide where to commit yourself. What goals are most important for your wellbeing? Find ways to say "NO" to the things and people who drain you of your energy and efforts.

Here are some commitment helpers to keep you on track.

Put it on paper. If you'll commit to writing out your goals, ideas, and dreams, you automatically give them more power in your mind.

Visualize the results you want. Use your imagination to 'feel' the results of what you are striving for. Imagination is a powerful tool. It connects you to infinite Spirit, infinite wisdom and supply. It also reinforces your commitment to the goal and gives you strength to continue.

Set small goals that lead you down the 'yellow brick road' to your success. It's easy to do little bits! Like adding water to a glass, one drop at a time, your efforts will eventually overflow.

Do something daily. Don't go to bed without having done SOMETHING that will lead to the success you seek.

Always give your best. Whatever you are doing, excellence is recognizable. Your commitment to excellence at every level will lead to the success you seek. It will draw people, events and resources toward you.

Time does not wait for you to commit to your success. Only you can decide whether to be great or mediocre. Hang on to your attitude and determine to succeed. Be patient with yourself, the people around you, and the process required to become successful. Commit today to achieve your best tomorrow!

SELF CONTROL

For me, the hardest part of trying to make changes in ones life is that little thing that we call self-control.

Ever made the decision to start exercising? You get all excited about it. You set the alarm clock to get up early the next morning so you can exercise 45 minutes before starting your day. The alarm clock goes off and what happens? You hit the snooze button. Aw, forget exercising. What were you thinking? The bed feels too good. You are simply too tired to get up. You will have to start another day.

Or perhaps you did get up that morning, and even the next. But three days into your program, the bed feels better than the idea of getting up and exercising.

What is the problem here?

The problem is - NO SELF CONTROL.

Or what about this?

You write out all of your goals. You make the decision to review your goals each day and actively work on them.

For five days, you do exactly that.

Then, the fifth day comes and you simply don't have the time to do it. The next day, you can't find the time to focus on your goals either. Hey, you have the big project that is due and there are the kids that have that meeting at their school that you must attend, and your spouse need help out in the garage. There are way too many things that you must do and focusing on your goals simply will have to take a back seat for the day.

Here's another example: You decide to read the book from cover to cover. You will do it each night before going to sleep--read two complete chapters before going to bed. For three days you do just that. The fourth day, you are too tired to read the book, so you fall to sleep.

Now, if any of this sound like you, don't feel bad. It sounds like most of us.

The problem is, most of us have absolutely no self-control.

In order to make the necessary changes you will have to make in order to create the life that you desire--a spirit filled life, a life on purpose, a life that is happy and stress free, you must learn self-control.

But how do you develop Self-Control?

Well, developing self-control requires a combination of a few things. See, most of us slip up when we decide to make changes and when we do back slide" we simply say, "Oh, well. I'll try harder next time." But when the next time comes, we slip up again.

Why? Because you have not come up with a plan. We have not truly made the decision to make the change we desire. Right now, it is just a desire. When you are truly serious about it, you will make THE DECISION. Once you make the decision, you will need a plan to carry it out. You will also need a lot of prayer. And you can't forget adding affirmations and visualization to make sure you stay on course with your self control.

What do I mean by a plan? You need to know EXACTLY what it is that you wish to do. Write it out. Say it out loud.

"I quit smoking."

Then, you will pray on it. Thank God for already giving you the thing that you desire.

"God I thank you for taking away my desire to smoke!"

Next, repeat your affirmations as often as you can. Tell everybody you know and meet.

"I do not smoke." "You know I quit smoking, don't you?" "I'm not a smoker."

Repeat it as often as you can so that you are always mindful of the fact that you are not a smoker.

Then, visualize yourself as smoke-free. Visualize yourself smelling your clothes and they are fresh. Visualize yourself turning down a cigarette that is offered to you. Visualize yourself running a marathon and not being out of breathe.

You may have to sacrifice certain things that you enjoy, whether it is time-consuming gadgets, hobbies or types of food and drink. Once you determine to follow your goal through you must make necessary changes. remember to analyze your results and find room for improvement. Celebrate your successes, no matter how small. It is about making progress in life that brings us the success we want and deserve.

TIME MANAGEMENT

"Give me six hours to chop down a tree and I will spend the first four sharpening the axe."

Abraham Lincoln

You can measure success with the amount to time you spend on (trying) becoming successful. The word 'trying' denotes and already failure approach to becoming successful.

To measure the time you have made towards your success in whatever business you have began whether it is on-line or a physical product you are promoting by breaking it down daily. You can do this by listing how much time you spend on:

- Sleeping (include naps)
- Eating (break it down and add breakfast-30 minutes, lunch 30 minutes, dinner 1.5 hrs)
- Working (8 hours, 6 hours?)
- Studying (whether it is in school or reading marketing books)
- Exercising
- Playing
- Watching television
- Serving others
- Praying/Meditating
- House maintenance (yard work, fixing things)
- Business

So, break this down daily to weekly. Be sure to include the weekends. From this you will see how much time is actually spent on your business building. Is this enough?

Anyone can achieve success. The difficulty lies in changing your life; the time you spend on television, the time you spend sleeping, the time you spend working on the house or working to earn money. All of this time defines whom you are and in what direction you are taking your life or road to your ultimate destination.

Next, write out your ultimate destination. Do not put a date on it as if you do not make the date you may feel a failure. You are never a failure if you are continually pursuing your dream.

Now, how many hours per week are you spending on your business and what can you cut out of your weekly hours to contribute to your business? My one area I omitted completely in my life that has made a difference is: TELEVISION. Yes, I tossed my television and rely only on radio, newspaper and Internet for the news. That alone freed up a lot of time. Time I used to building my on-line business. I still kept the exercise, the time spent on my home, etc.

As I spent more time on my business I found that I did not miss television. I was well entertained staying in touch with any customers, developing new marketing strategies, looking at other sites to earn advertising credits. Yes, that takes up some time, but I would rather earn some free ads then watch a bunch of ads that earn me nothing but wasted time.

As you see where your time is spent you begin to see yourself in a new light and here is where you can begin to break the barriers of old habits, breaking the mental and emotional bonds that have tied you to mediocrity.

Yes, mediocrity. In the future you will not know what stars are breaking up, who is sleeping with whom. In the future I hope you will not care.

As you are spending more time on your business and not the business of others, you may find it hard to relate to these others. While you are talking business ideas they are talking lifestyles of the rich and famous. One day you may walk away. But don't let this discourage you. I still have friends that are not intrigued, interested or even mildly curious in what I am doing. And that is OK.

Eliminating television is just a start. There are other ways to increase your time on business building. The first is to ACT. MOVE. Get out of bed earlier; go to bed later. Successful people never let a day go by without moving closer to their goals; Even if it is an extra one ½ hour daily.

Sometimes in the beginning of your road to success you have to believe in Yourself. You really have to make the Effort to change your pattern of living. Much to the surprise of my uncle, when I first said, "No, I am not watching this movie tonight, I have to work" I began to change his perspective of what I am doing to accomplish my goals.

Now, this doesn't happen continually with always giving up your time with your family to achieve your financial goal. Once you find your actions are producing results, you can begin to relax on those rigorous hours you have set for yourself. This can take some time but the results are worth it.

When you are successful you and your family will automatically not be watching television as your entertainment you may be traveling instead. Is not that the Ultimate Goal?

SELECT THE RIGHT FRIENDS

"True friends stab you in the front."

Oscar Wilde

Regardless of how great you think you are, both the historical record and the basic laws of physics teach us that there is a limit as to what you can accomplish solely by yourself. If you are going to achieve great and significant things, you will at critical points need the motivational, physical and intellectual assistance of others.

The importance of friends was perhaps best stated over 2000 years ago by one of those anonymous wise men whose name has been lost to history: "Friends are God's way of taking care of us."

The people around whom you spend the bulk of your time will either be a benefit and enhancement to your life or they will be draining and retarding influences. Therefore, if you are sincerely looking to achieve great things in life, friendships, relationships and associations should not be left to chance. You have a personal responsibility to form mutually beneficial relations in order to better your life and achieve your individual greatness.

The secrets for finding and forming those relationships can be found in the basic laws of physics. Read them; act on them and succeed!

#1 - The First Law of Motion - We are indebted to the great physicist Sir Isaac Newton for this law. It is also known as the Law of Inertia because it basically states that an object will remain motionless or will keep moving in the same direction at the same speed (basically forever) unless acted upon by another force.

For our purposes here, this law basically states that you are not going to move forward or move forward at a faster pace unless you bring the right people (forces) into your life. In other words, you cannot do it all by yourself. By yourself, the best you can hope for is to move in a certain direction at a certain speed. If you what to change that direction or increase that speed, you must bring greater forces into your life. This includes greater knowledge and greater individual effort. But it also includes better and more beneficial friends.

#2 - The Law of Association - Other than the parents who raised you and instilled your core personality, the people who will have the greatest impact (positively and negatively) on your life are the people with whom you associate most frequently.

If you are not receiving maximum benefit from your current friends, then you need to begin associating with more uplifting and beneficial people. Go where beneficial people go: Their social clubs, their seminars, their meetings, their parties, their churches, etc. Identify the types of people which can be most beneficial to you and begin to associate with them directly. You can also associate with them indirectly by reading what they read: books, magazines, etc.

#3 - The Law of Radiant Energy - It is a physical law that all people radiate energy. Several years ago two Italian scientists calculated that each adult radiates energy roughly equivalent to that given off by a 75-watt light bulb.

Now, we are stretching things a bit here but we ask the question: What are you radiating? What message or aura do you send to others as you walk, talk and make your way through life? Do you speak with confidence, walk with pride, look good, smell good, etc? Are you someone with which others would want to associate? Remember, your radiant energy or aura attracts others, repels them or is neutral meaning you tend not to be noticed one way or the other.

You must work on and build an aura which attracts the type of people which can be beneficial to your life.

4 - The Law of Mutual Benefit - If someone is beneficial to you but you are not beneficial to them, then in a long term relationship with that person you

will begin to be viewed as a parasite. In order to avoid this situation and the disrespect which tends to result from it, you must make yourself valuable. Others should receive a benefit (intellectual, spiritual, practical, motivational) from associating with you.

Relationships founded upon mutual benefit tend to be the longest lasting and produce the most positive and constructive results. But here again, do not leave things to chance. Make yourself beneficial but also make sure others know about your benefits. You should not be a shameless self-promoter but through your conversations and writings you can make sure others know what you have to offer.

5 - E=mc squared - We are indebted to the genius Albert Einstein for this law. It states that energy (E) equals mass (m) times the speed of light squared (c squared). This law says a lot but for our purposes here, it says a small amount of mass can produce an enormous amount of energy. Indeed, this law is the theory behind the atomic bomb.

Energy is what enables us to accomplish things. As an individual (mass) you can produce an enormous amount of energy. But suppose for one moment you can multiply that energy production by having two or three like-minded people helping you achieve a goal. Friends increase your energy output and enable you to accomplish things way beyond that which can be achieved by you individually.

Friends are powerful.

YOU MUST HAVE COURAGE

"Boldness has genius, power, and magic in it. Begin it now."

Johann Wolfgang Von Goethe

A bold attitude will inspire you to seek out an entirely new range of oftentimes challenging experiences.

Feelings of boldness can influence the choices you make. You may feel compelled to step out of your comfort zone, personally or professionally, so that you can explore all that the world has to offer. In your zeal to enjoy new experiences, you might occasionally feel a sense of discomfort at being out of your element. This is part of the growth process. Your courage can sustain you as you immerse yourself in unfamiliar territory and struggle to learn who you truly are. If you feel lost or directionless, you can get back on track by seeking out a mentor/coach, who understands your quest for change.

Personal and professional growth tends to be uncomfortable precisely because it requires you to face challenges that are entirely new. While it is possible to make small leaps in evolution without broadening your horizons to the extreme, the progress you achieve will invariably be more profound when you remove yourself from your comfort zone in order to face the unknown head on. This requires faith on your part, as it will be rare that you are totally sure that your efforts to discover more about yourself and about the world around you will be met with total success. However, the rewards you eventually come to are frequently worth the temporary stress caused by your departure from all that you have embraced as fact in the past.

Success is the progressive realization of meaningful goals. This definition means that you will continually realize success one goal at a time with another goal waiting to be realized. Goals, by definition, are: measurable, achievable, observable and timely. you set your own goals and how to measure them.

Goals are quantitative; winning an award, meeting an earnings goal or sales quota, obtaining a new job or promotion, getting married, losing weight, pulling off an event you organized, taking a trip, learning a sport, etc. Or they can be qualitative; forgiving someone, facing a crises with tact, compassion, level headedness and leadership, or reaching out to others, changing a bad habit, improving communication or relationship skills, etc.

Quantitative and qualitative goals may be declared in every area of your life, and if they are important to you, they are how you create a meaningful life.

Courage is the greatest of all the virtues. Because if you haven't courage, you may not have an opportunity to use any of the others. --Samuel Johnson

BE OPEN MINDED

"Without an open-minded mind, you can never be a great success."

Martha Stewart

If you want to maximize your potential for success in business and in life, you've got to be open minded. Don't limit yourself - there are so many great things that you can do and accomplish if you open yourself to the world and open your eyes to the things that are available for you.

Perhaps you've become accustomed to some routines and patterns. You only see things in black and white because you've gotten used to this kind of thinking - just more of the same. However, despite what you perceive as commonplace in your everyday life and environment, if you're open minded, you'll definitely see more and allow more. Don't limit yourself to a small box and the small and ordinary ways of thinking.

Maximize your potential because you deserve more!

By limiting yourself, you're assuming that nothing else is going to happen, nothing is going to change, and that you're powerless. Do you ever think that way?

If you remain open minded to all of the possibilities in life, you'll see that life is so much more than some small place - opportunities are abundant. So if you wish to maximize your potential and truly make the most out of the opportunities that come your way, you should learn how to think out of the box by following these tips:

Rely on and trust yourself when making decisions. If you've become accustomed to relying on people for your actions, stop this practice. Instead, start making decisions for yourself. If you used to look up to someone for the things that you have to do, this is the time for you to take charge and take the lead to maximize your potential. It's now time for you to go out of your comfort zone and get out of your box.

Question things. Who said that you must accept things as they are? If something confuses you or you don't understand what's going on, don't hesitate to question it. If your ignorance and innocence is limiting your reach, it's especially important to remember to be open minded - spread your arms and your mind to widen your reach.

Learn to think beyond what is in front of you. When you deal with things, always view it not just in relation to what you have at the moment, but also to what it could bring for your future that could potentially help you maximize your potential. You need to understand that everything is connected, and your power to anticipate and think ahead, can and will make wonders for you.

Maximize your potential because you can!

Feel free to make mistakes. It's nice to take risks from time to time. If you're too frightened to move out of your box because you're afraid of making mistakes, you will never get to see what's outside. You may trip and you may fall. Don't worry about making a mistake. Instead, think of what you'll do when you get where you want to go.

Let other people inspire you. If you cannot see yourself going out of the box, then try to visualize yourself through other people's lives. Study other people's achievements and marvel at what they have accomplished. Let their achievements inspire you to achieve more for yourself. Believe that if they were able to do it, you can do it for yourself as well.

Continue learning. Explore other things that you've not tried before. Go places, try new adventures, learn and feed on your zest for knowledge because these things will broaden your horizon and allow you to go beyond what most people expect of you.

Open minded people have the greatest power to maximize their potential. It's all about thinking differently - getting out of the box that limits you. It's completely up to you. As you encounter people and discover programs that promise to help you maximize your potential, keep in mind that it's your responsibility to take action. Take what you're learning and make it your own. Your ultimate success depends on it!

MAKE YOURSELF HUMBLE

"Pride makes us artificial and humility makes us real."

Thomas Merton

No one likes working with someone who is arrogant, but you also have to stand your ground or you will be bullied around. So how do you go about keeping yourself apparently humble while maintaining a backbone? Because that really is a way to gain quick access to people and success.

Ask a lot of questions. This is one way to get your point across without telling someone that they should do something differently. Once someone starts to open up from your questions, they become emotionally available to new ideas or different ways of thinking about things. An important point needs to be made here however; YOU also need to be listening. Perhaps your 'great' idea isn't quite as wonderful as you think it is, and once they explain why they are going about something a certain way you might realize they have a valid position. All of this needs to be done with integrity and with an honest intent to have the best solution for everyone. That is where the true humility comes into this.

You should phrase things in a passive voice. It is much easier for someone in a position of authority to listen to their underlings if the ideas are not presented in a "how stupid are you not to have thought of this" attitude.

Example: "Do you know where the measuring tape is?" sounds a lot more helpful than, "Don't you think we thought to measure this board before we start cutting?"

Again, this needs to be sincere, and you need to keep this in mind when the shoe is on the other foot. The supervisor who ignores the thoughts and suggestions of his staff will not get support when he needs it.

Keep the big picture and the final result in the top of your mind. Why do you need to press a certain point? Is it to demonstrate your knowledge and expertise on the subject? Will your way make a significant difference in the long term? Why are you bringing a particular issue up at a certain time? Sometimes suggestions offered in private are more readily accepted than those given in front of a group. It can be a matter of 'face' rather than practicality in many instances.

Lastly, don't take rejection of an idea as a rejection of you personally. Maybe your way is not significantly better than another way, and the groundwork is already done on the current solution, where your point may require rework that isn't in the budget or within time constraints.

In order to make progress in your life you have to commit to making change. If you don't make changes tomorrow is going to be very similar to yesterday, with the exception of you being a day older.

BE A SELF STARTER

"Today will never happen again. Don't waste it with a false start or no start at all."

Og Mandino

Self-starters are the ones you go to if you want to get things done, right now!

Working in the home business arena, I always look for self-starters to partner with me. They require little to no supervision or direction to achieve their objective. They can motivate themselves in any direction and don't have to be prompted to take ACTION. They take initiative, work smart, and just get on with doing whatever it takes to get things done. Neither do they quit if things don't go to plan on the first attempt. In fact, they'll go the extra mile.

You see, like Ann Sieg, I too work within a space that requires me to use my brain a little.

Self-starters are entrepreneurs that realize that success requires WORK. But the difference between wanting to be successful and actually being successful is all in the drive. Self-starters are highly motivated by the innate desire to succeed. They don't dillydally around waiting for things to happen, but aspire to be the best and apply their determination to take them there.

Self-starters love a challenge, they are confident in tackling their work in the right away. It doesn't overwhelm them and they quickly carry out what they set out to achieve.

SELF RELIANT

"Nothing at last is sacred but the integrity of your own mind."

Ralph Waldo Emerson

when you don't have to rely on someone else, you are the master of your own destiny. That's really the secret to everything in life. If you're OK with yourself and you don't need others approval for your happiness, then you are happy. Self reliance comes with self confidence. Self reliance helps a person to prepare for life challenges. Rest your mind and imagine a situation where you are confident and successful. Go over the details thoroughly in your mind. What did you do? What did you say? You can also try to remember a time in the past when you acted with a lack of confidence. Go over the situation in your mind, changing whatever details you would need to alter the outcome to a desired one.

Visualize yourself strengthening your self-confidence and acting the way you wish you would have acted. Don't judge yourself - simply re-create the situation and envision yourself with strong self-confidence, and having the outcome be better. To build on self improvement one needs to love him/herself. Leaning to love yourself is fundamental in self improvement and building good self esteem. You need to improve yourself by first understanding yourself and accepting the way you are. Self improvement brings happiness and satisfaction to one's life.

Though the road to self improvement is not easy, it is compulsory for one to experience happiness in life. When you stop and deal with your issues and insecurities, you are on the road to a more well and vibrant you and hence achieving success will be easy.

YOU ARE RESPONSIBLE FOR YOUR ACTIONS

"If you take responsibility for yourself you will develop a hunger to accomplish your dreams."

Les Brown

What do you think of when you contemplate the word responsible? I want you to be honest with yourself here. Do you secretly wish you weren't responsible for as much as you are? Are you trying to get out of responsibilities because they're just "too much"? Have you been unrealistic about how much you can commit to and still uphold your responsibilities? Do you find yourself blaming others for things that don't go your way?

I believe for entrepreneurs, responsibility can be a very loaded term. Let's face it, we all want to feel responsible for our successes when they occur, but it's no fun taking responsibility for your failures, too. But, alas, this is part of the conscious entrepreneur's journey; being awake and aware to both sides of the coin when it comes to responsibility.

The truth is responsibility isn't a very "hot" or "sexy" topic. Responsibility brings you face to face with the more challenging aspects of being an entrepreneur. I learned this the hard way by having gone through a few failures in my past. Both with my Event management and Packaging. Both of these businesses had a certain level of success, but not enough to be sustainable over the long run and I had to shut them down. It was painful to look at the truth that I was responsible for what happened with those businesses.

Granted, if I had them both to do over again today, I would change many things and I see exactly how I'd set those businesses up for long-term success. But, I have no intention of starting these business over again at this point, but I do feel I can share some thoughts that may help you feel fantastic about being responsible for your own success.

Here are three key considerations for loving your responsibilities... and owning them fully:

Don't Bite Off More Than You Can Chew

This is one of the most pressing issues I see with entrepreneurs. It's so easy for us to get excited about many, many things. Often entrepreneurs will bite off more than they can chew. The reason many business owners do this is because they don't realize how much effort will go into a particular project. They make their timelines too short, their goals too aggressive and then get overwhelmed and discouraged when a project takes a long time and doesn't reach it's goals.

I'm taking my own advice into consideration and releasing a few projects that I just don't have the time, or energy to do right now. I had bitten off more than I could chew. The important thing here is to try not do to this in the first place, but if you do you've got to take steps to recognize you've committed to too much, and make some adjustments so you feel you don't have too much on your plate.

Hear What People Are Saying To You

Another mistake entrepreneurs make is a totally unconscious response of not hearing what people are telling you. This is easy to do when you're excited about something and you want to live in the "honeymoon" of your idea. This is an intoxicating state of bliss, and it's challenging to get grounded into some of the input you're getting on your project.

This happened to me with my Event management group. I kept hearing from people at the meetings that it was something very special, and I better prepare myself for rapid growth. I didn't listen. I didn't want to complicate things. I didn't want the responsibility of running yet another business when the one I already had was struggling. So, I embarked on a "stop gap" approach to that business, rather than hearing what everyone told me in the beginning. Had I only "heard" what they said, I'm sure that business would be thriving today. So, if you notice you're doing this in your business...

letting important input go in one ear and out the other like you never even heard it... listen up! This is the Universe speaking to you through the people you've placed in your life. It's worth paying full attention to what they're saying, because their input may be guiding you toward taking on your responsibility with a lot more ease, grace and fun!

Notice if You're Placing Blame on Others

This one is a big tell-tale sign that you don't want to take responsibility for your own success. This one isn't particularly fun to look at, but it is extraordinarily valuable to do this self-evaluation. Simply notice... is there something in your business or your life that isn't working right now. Identify what that is, and see if you are placing blame on someone else for the situation you are in.

Believe me, I understand that sometimes things happen to you, but even then, how you respond (versus react) is your responsibility. How you learn from a situation and use it to discover more about yourself and your relationship to responsibility can make a huge impact on your success. Everything that occurs in your business is a learning opportunity... remember every single thing that happens is happening for one purpose and one purpose only; because the Universe is conspiring for your highest and best at all times. Even those situations where you want to blame; chances are those are the places you have the greatest gifts waiting for you.

When you take these three concepts into consideration in your business, you'll find it much easier be fully engaged and happy in your commitments. You'll also feel confident that you can be (and WANT to be) responsible for your own success. This is one of the most exciting aspects of being a conscious entrepreneur; there's nobody that can create your success, but you. Yes, of course, you have coaches, consultants and mentors to help you along the way, but ultimately your success is up to you.

BE A LISTENER

"The art of effective listening is essential to clear communication, and clear communication is necessary to management success."

James Cash Penney

"How can I succeed?" As intelligent, ambitious students, many of you spend lots of time considering which classes and specific skills — from coding to Spanish language — will bring you the most career success. But there are certain less-obvious skills that underpin success in nearly all careers — among the most important are listening and communication.

Learning to read another person's face, understand their perspective and truly synthesize what they're saying (rather than just waiting for your turn to speak) will you allow to better collaborate in your study group, project team, political action committee, traveling troupe of acrobats, or wherever else you wish to go in life.

So, in short…

Don't be like Simon.

Instead, learn...

10 Ways to Get Your Listen On.

Here is a list of 10 ways that will help you become a more effective listener.

- Face the speaker and maintain eye contact

- Be attentive, but relaxed
- Keep an open mind
- Listen to the words and try to picture what the speaker is saying
- Don't interrupt and don't impose your "solutions"
- Wait for the speaker to pause to ask clarifying questions
- Ask questions only to ensure understanding
- Try to feel what the speaker is feeling
- Give the speaker regular feedback
- Pay attention to what isn't said—to nonverbal cues

BUILD A STRONG NETWORK

"Networking is an essential part of building wealth. "

Armstrong Williams

You may already be aware of the power of a powerful network. People with the right connections hear about internships and job opportunities before anyone else does. Even in the toughest job market, they're the ones who land the best positions in the most prestigious firms. The right connections can matter more than background, location, age, appearance, gender, or social status. People who have a wealth of quality connections can access the kinds of opportunities and resources that lead to greater success. The right connections are worth their weight in gold.

The Four Key Beliefs of Successful Connectors

#1: All business relationships are relationships first. As InfusionSoft CEO Clate Mask says, "I'm not interested in developing 'business relationships'; I want to create relationships on a deeper level." Relationships are about building connections with others who feel you have their best interests at heart, and vice versa. You must enter into every business relationship seeking to get to know the other person and, if possible, help them out.

#2: Relationships are about giving and receiving value. In all relationships—with your local mailman, your favorite professor, your little sister, your mother, and even with a stranger you interact with in a grocery store—you are giving and receiving value constantly. Power connecting is based upon consistently adding value to other people, and receiving their assistance in return.

#3: Relationships must be authentic on both sides. People must know you, like you, and trust you before they will do business with you, and for that to happen, you must be authentic, honest, and trustworthy. The people you bring into your network must have the same qualities. Your network is your most prized possession; make sure it's composed of only the best individuals. Be on the lookout for bad actors and unreliable people. Measure the value of your contacts not by their net worth but by whether they have a good head, heart, and gut.

#4: To be successful, your network must be wide, deep, and robust. It's sometimes tempting to seek out only people who are like us, or who are in the same profession, for our network. But the true power of business relationships often comes from connecting people from diverse and divergent spheres with each other. Successful people have relationships in finance, media, politics, and their communities, as well as in their industries and families. This gives them access to information and opportunities they would never have otherwise.

With these four beliefs, you can start to build a strong, powerful network even before you enter the workforce. However, you also must conscientiously avoid five pitfalls that will diminish your relationship-building efforts.

The Five Pitfalls of the Inefficient Connector

#1: Networking in the wrong places for what they need. Networking will help only if you are searching for the people in the right places. Your favorite nightclub, coffee shop or gym may not be locations where the people you need to meet are hanging out. On the other hand, the alumni association or an upcoming tech conference might give you access to the person who will give you your next job or important contact.

#2: Networking at the wrong level for their goals. Instead of connecting with individuals and organizations that can provide the high-level support, direction, and connections they need, most people spend too much time with those at their own level of knowledge and skill, or lower. Your friends are great for support, but you need to reach "up and out" to make contact with people who can guide, mentor, and open doors for you.

#3: Not assessing the relative value of their connections. College students and recent grads have the constant urge to connect with others via social media or through numerous social events. But the truth is, there are only so many hours in the day and so much time in our lives to effectively maintain relationships. (Social science research states that we can effectively keep track of only around 150 people at a time.) You have to appreciate the value of every connection while determining exactly what assistance that connection brings to you and what assistance you can give in return.

#4: Not using a system to optimize their networking efforts. Handing out thousands of business cards or resumes probably won't get you the job of your dreams. Meeting lots of useful people and then not having the courage or taking the time to follow up professionally won't accelerate your plans either. You must systematically connect and then build relationships over time.

#5: Failing to create high-value, long-term connections. The key isn't the number of contacts you make: it's the number of contacts that turn into long-lasting connections. Relationships can't be built overnight. You must commit to helping others consistently, adding value appropriately, and connecting them with other people who may help them out as well. The strongest relationships are based upon consistent added value.

The right network doesn't have to be inherited. You don't have to attend a prestigious university, or have your family endow a new library addition. Your uncle or family friends doesn't have to run a Fortune 500 company for you to be able to find and build strong connections with people who could help you with your life and business goals. All it takes is a few, simple skills, learned well and applied consistently, to create the kind of power connections that will accelerate your success.

WORK ETHIC

"Everyone talks about age, but it's not about age. It's about work ethic. Winning never gets old."

Lisa Leslie

No matter what you do, developing a good work ethic is absolutely key to your success. Having one increases the possibility of promotion and of retention in tough economic times. Maintaining a good work ethic is easy:

Be on time. In fact, be a little early, especially for appointments, but always be on time for work. Every day. Factor in the time it usually takes you to get from home to your work, find parking, and get to wherever you need to be at the beginning of your work day, and then add 10 to 15 extra minutes to give you a cushion. Getting to work late every day sends the message that you don't care, and that you're not committed to your job. Moreover, it builds resentment among co-workers and teammates who are getting to work on time.

Be professional. This goes far beyond dressing appropriately for your work. Practice having a positive attitude, and be cordial to everyone you meet during the workday. Don't engage in gossip, and be respectful to everyone around you. Most importantly, practice integrity. Work to be the person who can be look up to, and be honest, always acting the same way when alone, just as you do when others are watching you.

Be self-disciplined. Anything worth doing takes focus, and workplaces can be full of distractions. Keep your goals in mind, and train yourself to be persistent and to complete all projects. If it helps, make daily and weekly lists of tasks to be accomplished, and mark each task off as you complete it.

Making lists will also help you to break down and organize your tasks to help ensure you complete them on time. Above all, always try to do better than your best on any assignment.

Manage your time. If you can do it today, do it – don't put it off. Make note of how much time it takes you to complete certain tasks, and develop the ability to accurately estimate the time needed to complete projects. This will allow you to allocate enough time to do what you need to, and help to make the most of the working hours.

Take care of yourself. Get as much sleep as you need, every night. Take time to exercise regularly, and eat properly. Also keep in mind that burn out is very real, and helps no one. Take time to relax and recharge, where you don't think about work, or check your e-mail. Making sure that you enjoy life will help you keep your perspective at work, and make you a more productive employee.

Investing time and effort in developing a good work ethic is well worth it, and is often the extra edge in getting – and keeping – the job.

FINAL THOUGHT

Warren Buffett is successful for investing and building long-term businesses. Bill Gates is successful for creating a software empire that has changed the way we use computers. Gandhi was successful for leading India into independence from the British.

Success comes in many ways and forms. What's interesting is that most successful people have very similar qualities.

When I read lists such as this one, I want to see how I stack up against it. It feels good when I recognize qualities of success in myself. For the qualities that I don't have, lists like these tell me what I need to work on.

I have enjoyed and benefited much from these types of lists and that's why I decided to organize all my research, observations and experience and compile this comprehensive list.

If you want to achieve your life's dream and be wildly successful, you need to model yourself after people who are living their dream. The more qualities you have in common, the higher your chances for being wildly successful.

If you don't see all of these traits in yourself, don't worry! Successful people recognize that they don't know everything, but they are willing to keep growing and developing their skills. Becoming successful is within your grasp, if you're willing to put in the hard work to get there. Don't quit

ABOUT THE AUTHOR

Hi guys, my name is **Krishna Medge**, and i am from India

I have struggled many years as an entrepreneur to be successful in business and many of my business failed because there was no one to support me when I was younger. I tried new business, new ideas, but all didn't go well. I have a poor performance when I was in college and I didn't graduate until now. But all these setbacks never kept me away from achieving my goals. I keep on learning and taking knowledge, observing the successful people and learning from them

Finally, at the age of 21, I am now an entrepreneur with a successful business and investments in various streams.